Contents

Unit 1	Revising the ladder family	4
Unit 2	Revising the rubber ball family	6
Unit 3	Revising the cog family	8
Unit 4	Revising the cog cousins	10
Unit 5	Revising the zip wire family	12
Unit 6	Capital letters with straight lines	14
Unit 7	Capital letters with curves	16
Unit 8	Capital letters with straight lines and curves	18
Unit 9	Capital letters with sloping lines	20
Unit 10	Capital letters with straight and sloping lines	22
Unit 11	The numbers 1, 4, 7	24
Unit 12	The numbers 0, 6, 8, 9	26
Unit 13	The numbers 2, 3, 5	28
Unit 14	Punctuation focus	30
Unit 15	Capital and lowercase letters	32
WriteWell challenge 1		34
WriteWell challenge 2		35

Revising the ladder family

These letters are in the ladder family. They all start going straight down like the letter **l**.

To write these letters, always start at the top of the letter and go straight down the ladder.

l i t j u y

Try it

1 Trace and continue the pattern.

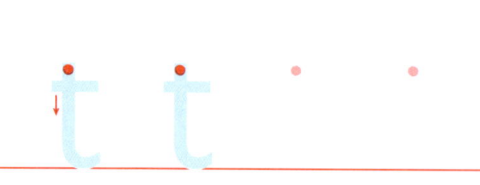

2 Trace each letter. Then write two of your own.

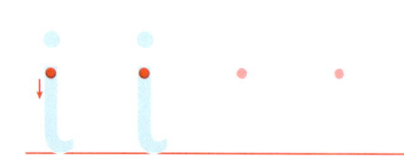

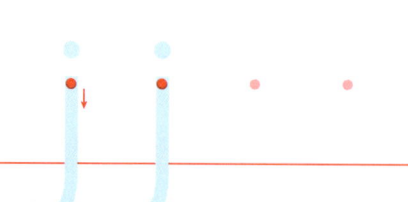

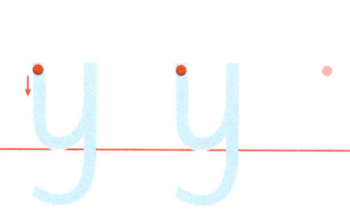

Practise it

Write each letter four times.

l   t

i   j

u   y

Apply it

Trace the word to complete each sentence.

Beth feels ill.

The match is lit.

Pay at the till.

I had a red lolly.

This jelly wobbles.

I like to jump.

Book 4 I Capital Letters and Numbers

Revising the rubber ball family

These letters are in the rubber ball family. They all start going down and then come back up and curve over like the letter **r**.

To write these letters, drop down, then bounce back up like a rubber ball and curve over.

r n m p h b k

Try it

1 Trace and continue the pattern.

2 Trace each letter. Then write two of your own.

Practise it

Write each letter four times.

n　　　　　　　　　m

h　　　　　　　　　b

k　　　　　　　　　p

Apply it

Write a word to complete each sentence.

rip　nip　pink　hump　brim

A pig is _____.

Card can _____.

A crab can _____.

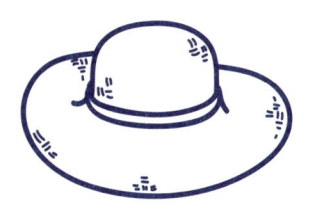

This hat has a _____.

A camel has a _____.

Book 4 I Capital Letters and Numbers

Revising the cog family

These letters are in the cog family. They all start like a letter **c** and curl round.

To write these letters, always curve over the top of the cog and curl round.

c o a d g q

Try it

1 Trace and continue the pattern.

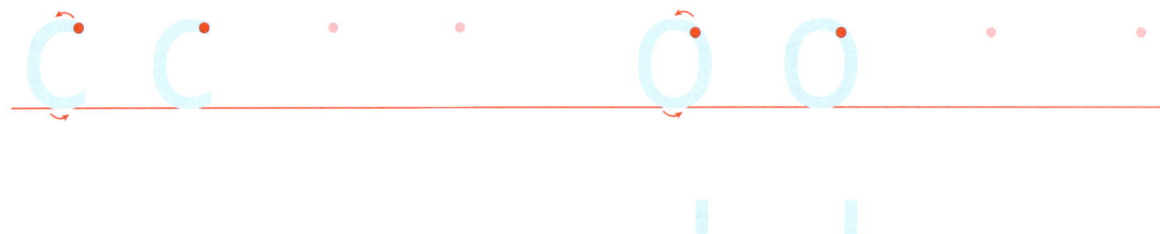

c c c c c

2 Trace each letter. Then write two of your own.

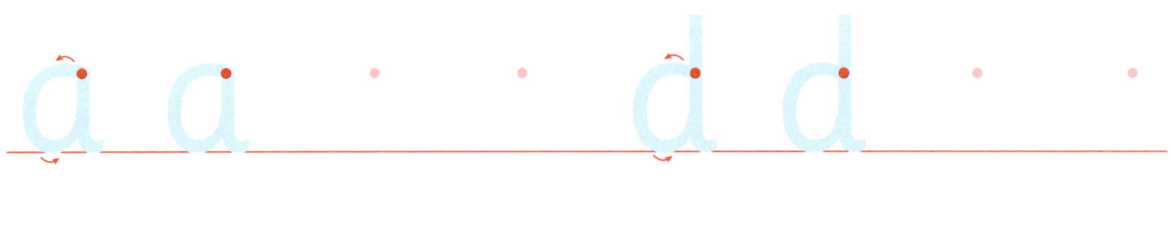

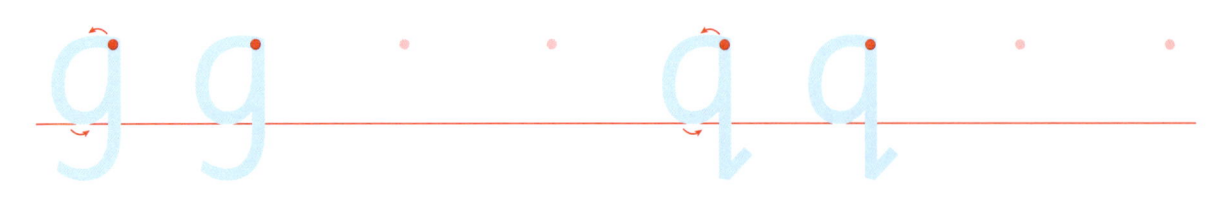

c c   o o

a a   d d

g g   q q

Practise it

Write each letter four times.

c					o

a					d

g					q

Apply it

Write a word to complete each sentence.

cog   dog   good   add   quack

This is my _____.

Ducks can _____.

This is a _____.

I can _____.

I am a _____ singer.

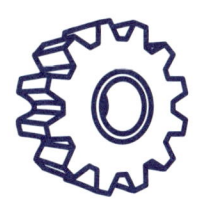

Book 4 | Capital Letters and Numbers

Revising the cog cousins

These letters are the cog cousins. They all have curves like the cog family but each cog cousin curves in a special way.

When you write the cog cousins, remember where each letter starts and how it curves.

s e f

Try it

1 Trace and continue the patterns.

2 Trace each letter. Then write two of your own.

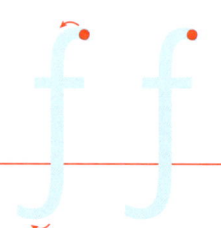

Practise it

Write each letter 10 times.

s

f

e

Apply it

Write a word to complete each phrase.

seek feet off puffs kiss

hands and

huffs and

on and

hide and

a hug and

Revising the zip wire family

These letters are in the zip wire family. They all have a sloping line like the letter **z**.

When you write these letters, your lines should always slope down from the top of the letter to the bottom like a zip wire.

Z V W X

Try it

1 Trace and continue the patterns.

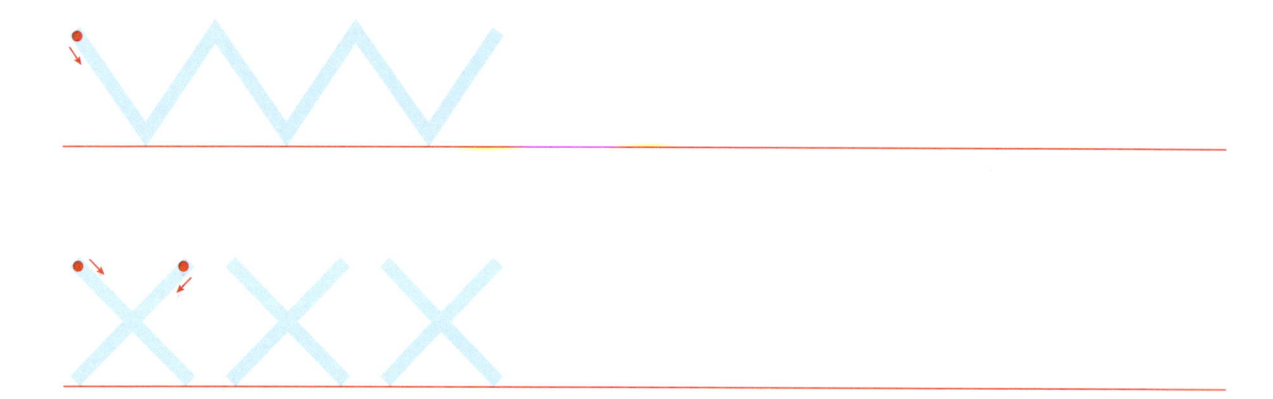

VVV

X X X

2 Trace each letter. Then write two of your own.

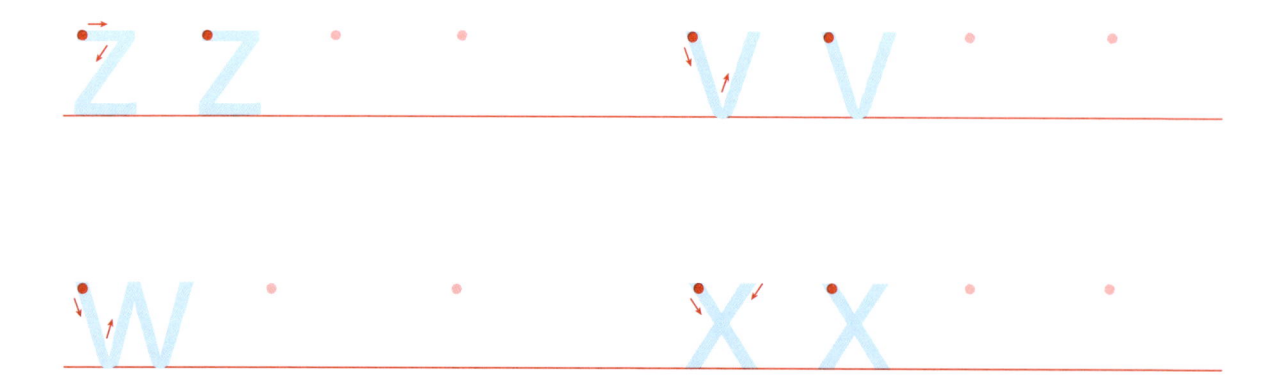

Z Z · ·   V V · ·

W · ·   X X · ·

Practise it

Write each letter four times.

Z   X

V   W

Apply it

Write a word to complete each phrase.

zero   two   twelve
    six   seven

_____ hands

_____ days

_____ months

_____ eggs

_____ one, two, three

Book 4 I Capital Letters and Numbers

Capital letters with straight lines

These capital letters are made up of straight lines.

To write these letters, always start at the top and draw a straight line down. Then add the lines across.

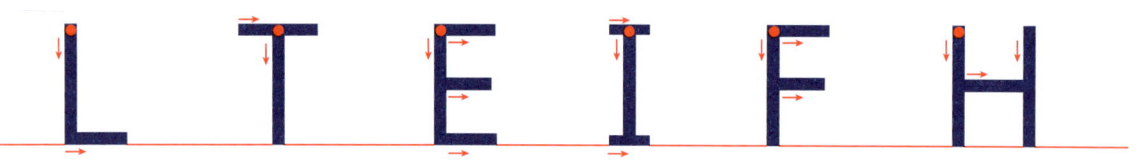

L T E I F H

Try it

1 Trace and continue the pattern of straight lines.

2 Trace each capital letter. Then write one of your own.

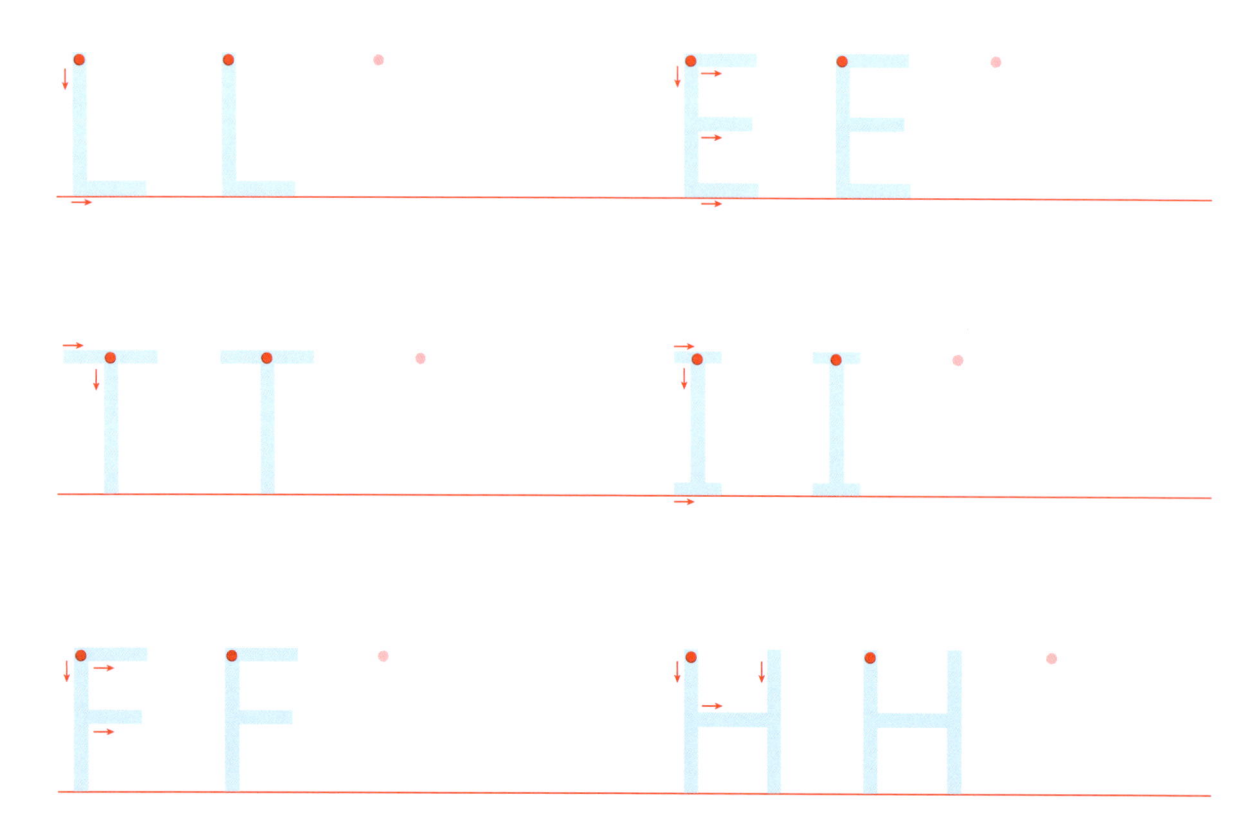

L L   E E

T T   I I

F F   H H

Practise it

Write each capital letter four times.

L . . . . E . . . .

T . . . . I . . . .

F . . . . H . . . .

Apply it

Copy the children's names. Remember to start names with a capital letter.

Liz　　　　Hasan　　　　Ella

Finn　　　　Tomas　　　　Isabel

Book 4 | Capital Letters and Numbers

Capital letters with curves

These capital letters are made up of curved lines.

To write these letters, always start at the top, curve over and then curl round.

C O Q G S

Try it

1. Trace and continue the pattern of curves.

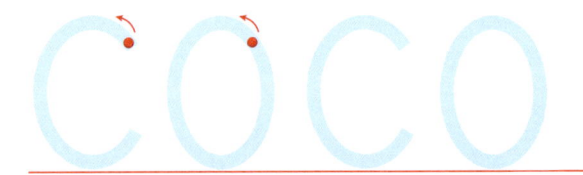

   C O C O

2. Trace each capital letter. Then write one of your own.

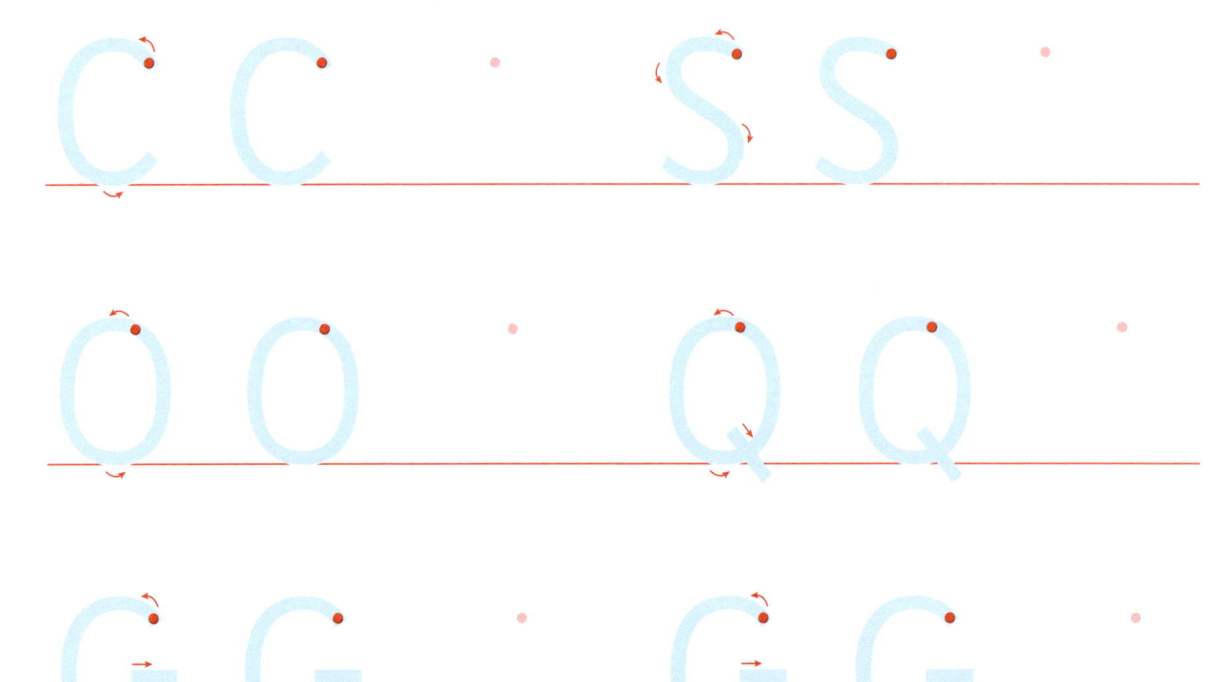

   C C   S S

   O O   Q Q

   G G   G G

Practise it

Write each capital letter four times.

C   S

O   Q

G   G

Apply it

Write the names of the people and places to complete each sentence.

Mr **Scott Quinn**
3 Main Street
Cardiff

Mrs **Carmel Garner**
7 High Street
Oxford

Mr _____

lives in _____ .

Mrs _____

lives in _____ .

Book 4 | Capital Letters and Numbers   17

Capital letters with straight lines and curves

These capital letters are made up of straight lines and curves.

Always start with the straight line down. Then curve for the letters **J** and **U**. To write the letters **D**, **B**, **P** and **R**, lift your pencil, go back to the top and add the curves.

D B P R J U

Try it

1 Trace and continue the pattern of straight lines and curves.

D D D

2 Trace each capital letter. Then write one of your own.

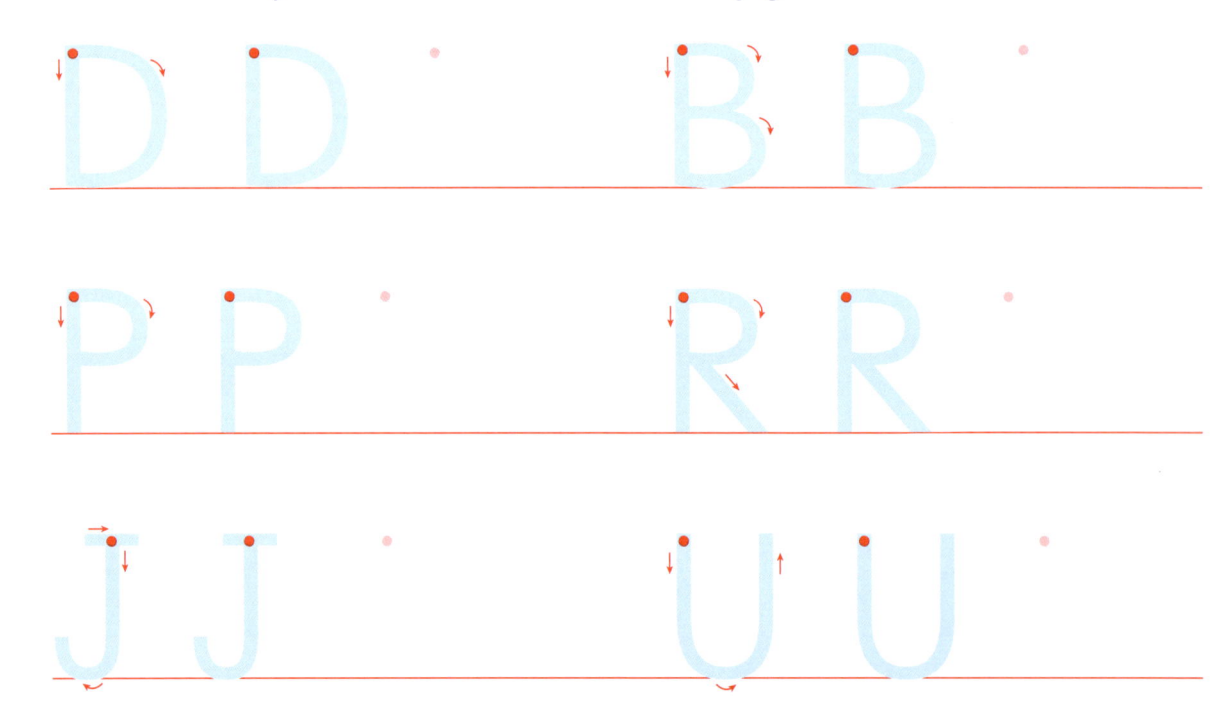

D D B B

P P R R

J J U U

18 Schofield & Sims WriteWell

Practise it

Write each capital letter four times.

D   B

P   R

J   U

Apply it

Look at the map. Write the word to complete each place name.

Green _____

Ash _____

_____ Pool

_____ Lane

_____ Street

Oak _____

Book 4 | Capital Letters and Numbers   19

Capital letters with sloping lines

These capital letters are made up of sloping lines.

To write these letters, always start at the top and slope down. Slope back up for the letters **V**, **W** and **Y**. Go back to the top and slope down the other way for the letters **A** and **X**.

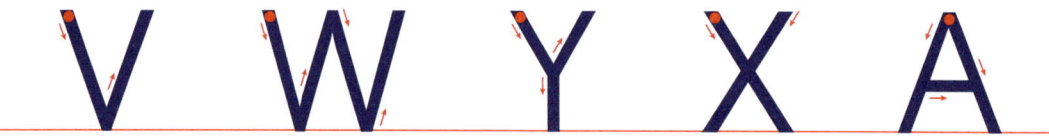

V W Y X A

Try it

1 Trace and continue the pattern of sloping lines.

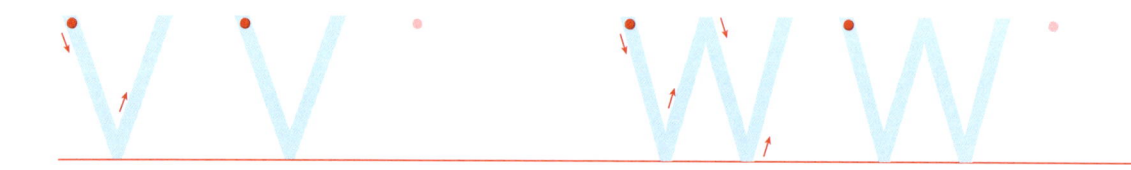

2 Trace each capital letter. Then write one of your own.

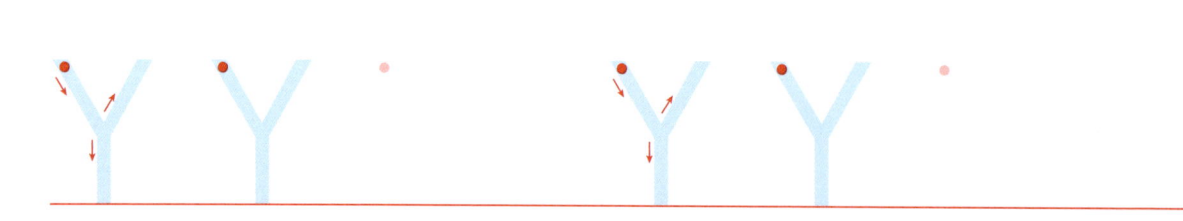

20

Schofield & Sims WriteWell

Practise it

Write each capital letter four times.

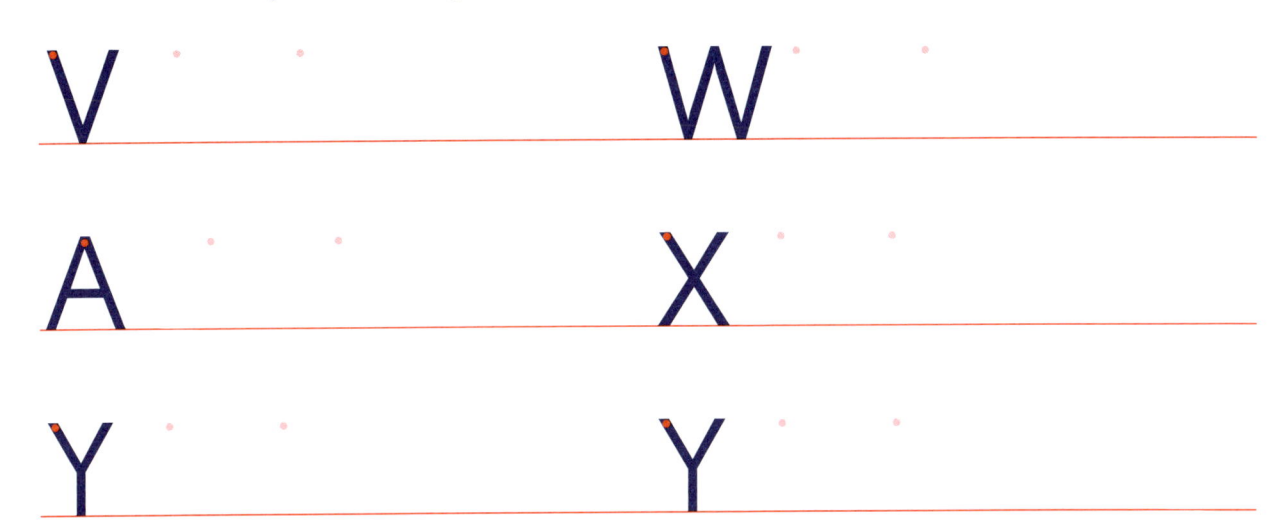

V

W

A

X

Y

Y

Apply it

Write the name of each teacher.

Mr Willis

Mr

Ms Vickers

Ms

Mrs Atkins

Mrs

Mrs Wali

Mrs

Mr Yang

Mr

Miss Allen

Miss

Book 4 | Capital Letters and Numbers

Capital letters with straight and sloping lines

These capital letters are made up of straight and sloping lines.

To write these letters, always start at the top. Start with a straight line and then add the sloping lines.

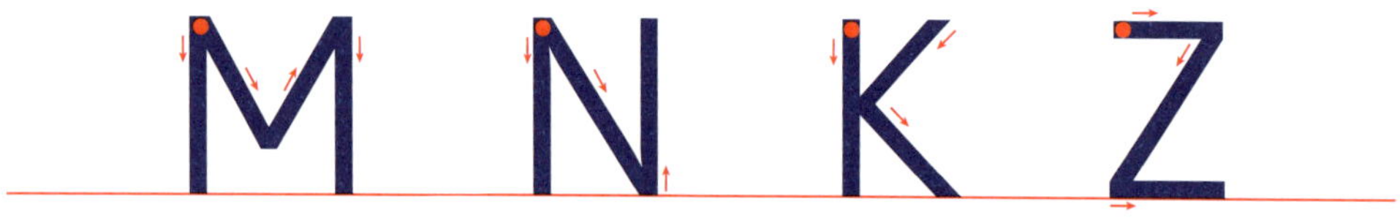

M N K Z

Try it

1 Trace and continue the patterns of straight and sloping lines.

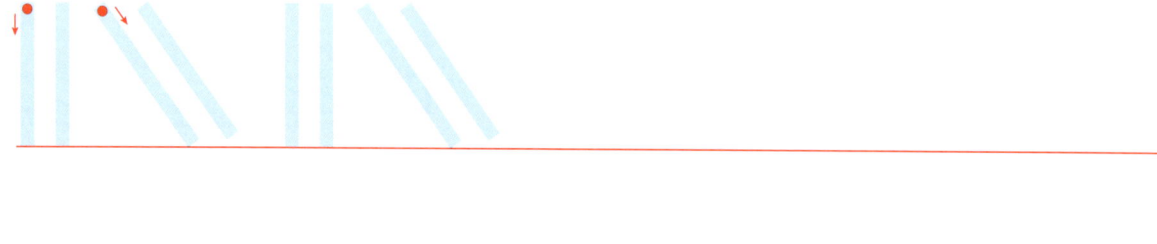

2 Trace each capital letter. Then write one of your own.

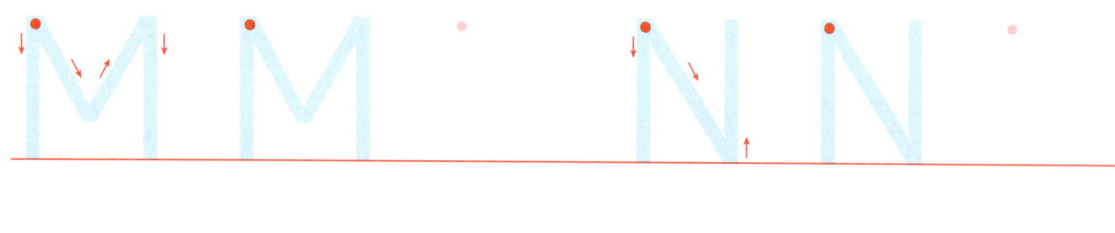

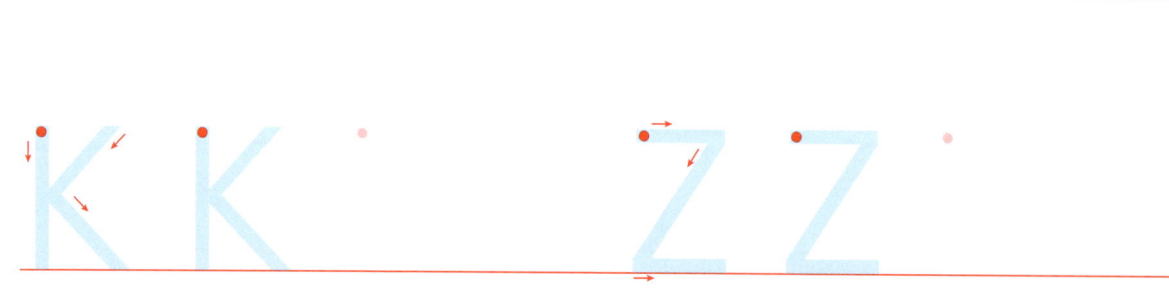

22

Schofield & Sims WriteWell

Practise it

Write each capital letter four times.

M   N

K   Z

Apply it

Write a word to complete each sentence.

Now   My   Zak   Kate   Mum

_____ name is Ben.

_____ is my sister.

_____ is my friend.

_____ I am six.

_____ says I am clever.

Book 4 | Capital Letters and Numbers

The numbers 1, 4, 7

These numbers are made up of straight and sloping lines.

To write the numbers **4** and **7**, start at the top and make a straight line. To write the number **1**, slope up to the top and go straight down.

1 4 7

Try it

1 Trace and continue the pattern of straight and sloping lines.

// + // +

2 Trace each number. Then write three of your own.

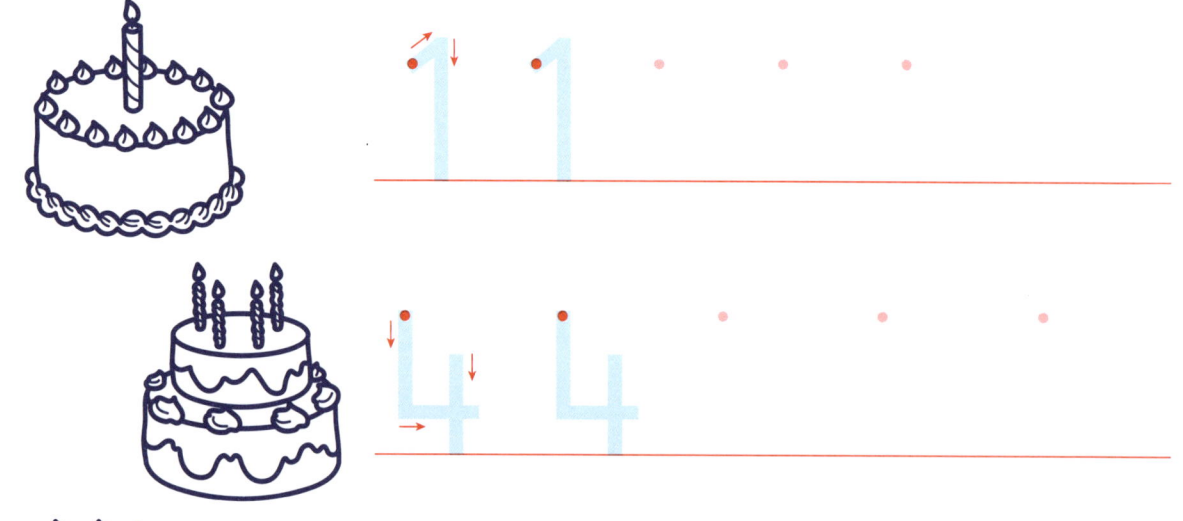

1 1

4 4

7 7

Practise it

Write each number 10 times.

1

4

7

Apply it

Write the number to complete each sentence.

Fatima is __ years old.

Ben is __ today.

Tess is __ years old.

I live at number __.

I am in Class __.

I play number __.

Book 4 I Capital Letters and Numbers

The numbers 0, 6, 8, 9

These numbers are made up of curved lines.

To write these numbers, always start at the top and curve round.

0 6 8 9

Try it

1 Trace and continue the pattern of curves.

0 8 0 8

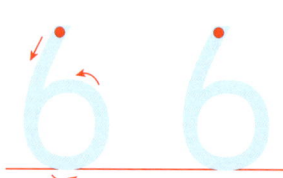

2 Trace each number. Then write three of your own.

0 0

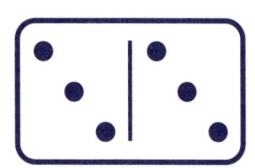

6 6

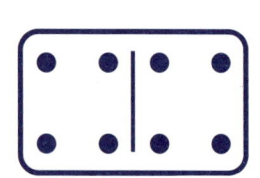

8 8

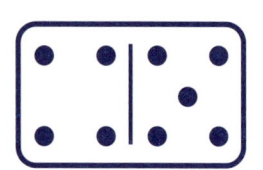

9 9

Practise it

Write each number 10 times.

0

6

8

9

Apply it

Write the numbers to complete each caption.

__ legs and __ spots

__ legs and __ spots

__ legs and __ spots

__ legs and __ spots

Book 4 I Capital Letters and Numbers

The numbers 2, 3, 5

These numbers are made up of backward curves like this:

To write the numbers **2** and **3**, start with the curve. To write the number **5**, go straight down and then curve round.

2 3 5

Try it

1 Trace and continue the pattern of curves.

2 Trace each number. Then write three of your own.

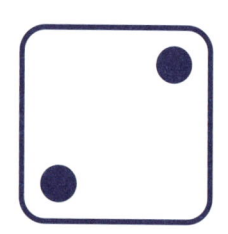

2 2

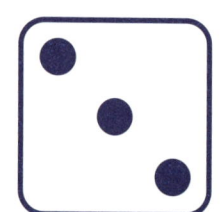

3 3

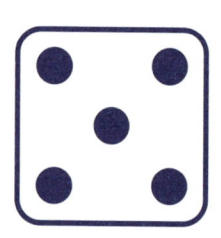

5 5

Practise it

Write each number 10 times.

2

3

5

Apply it

Write the numbers and trace the ending **s** to complete the shopping list.

___ sweet buns ✓

___ yummy cakes ✓

___ big lemons ✓

___ red plums ✓

___ jars of jam ✓

___ tins of beans ✓

Book 4 | Capital Letters and Numbers

Punctuation focus

Question marks and exclamation marks are punctuation marks. They both end with a small dot like a full stop.

To write these punctuation marks, start at the top and go down. Then make the dot underneath.

question mark **?**   exclamation mark **!**   full stop **.**

Try it

1 Trace and continue the patterns of lines and dots.

2 Trace each punctuation mark. Then write three of your own.

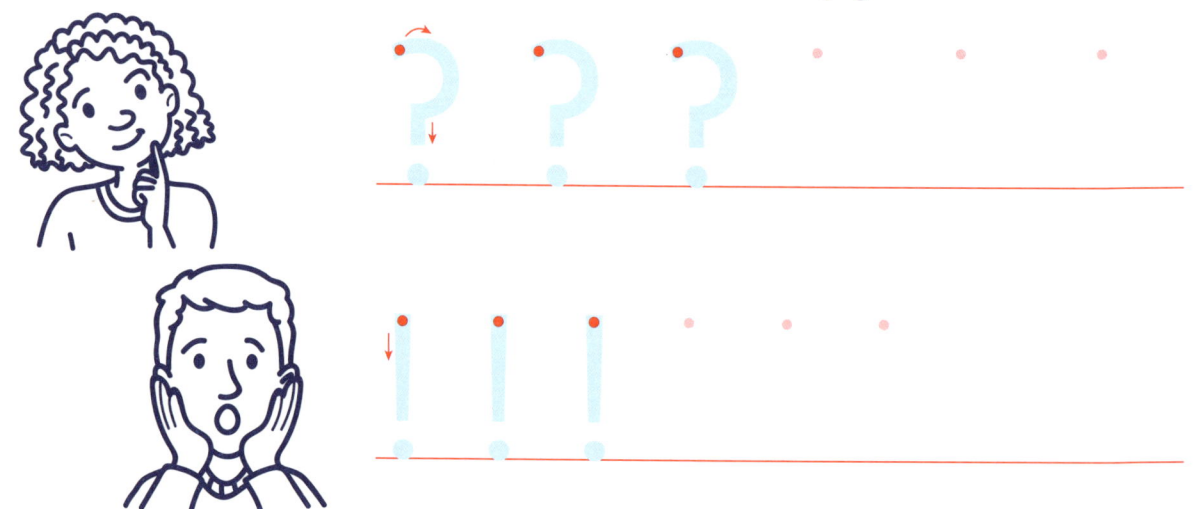

Practise it

Write each punctuation mark 10 times.

?

!

.

Apply it

Write the missing punctuation marks.

No_ Go away_

Help us_

Can I come in_

What do you want_

Book 4 | Capital Letters and Numbers 31

Capital and lowercase letters

Each letter has a capital letter shape and a lowercase shape. Some capital letters are the same shape as their lowercase letters. The capital letter is always bigger.

capital letters **A B C**   lowercase letters **a b c**

Try it

1 Trace and write the lowercase letters to complete the alphabet.

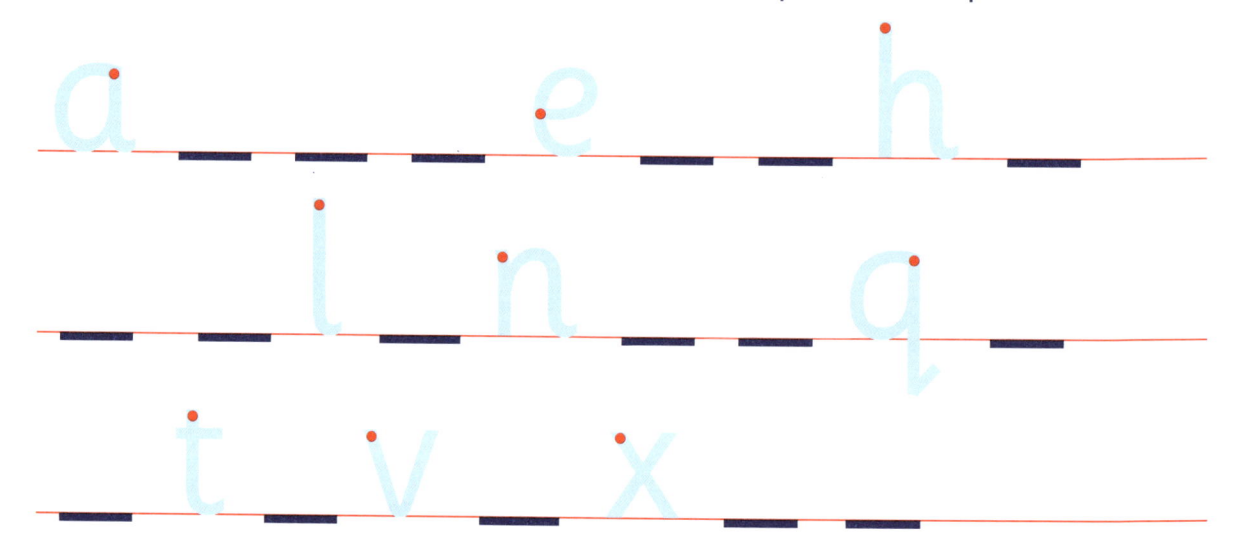

a _ _ e _ h
_ _
_ l _ n _ q
_ _
t _ v _ x
_

2 Trace and write the capital letters to complete the alphabet.

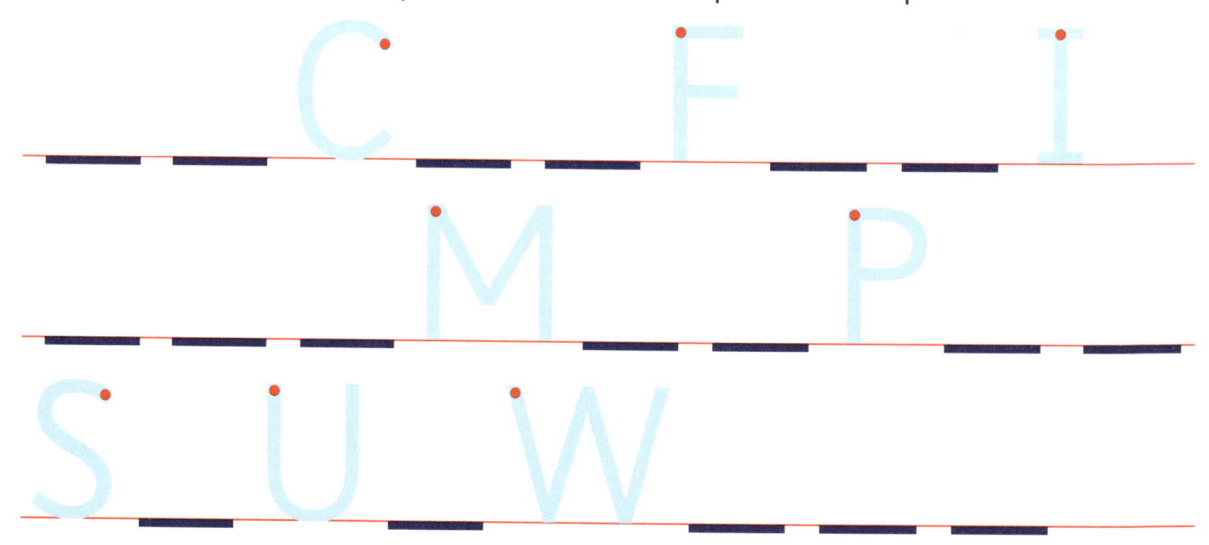

_ C _ F _ I
_ _ _
_ M _ P _
_ _ _
S _ U _ W _

Practise it

1 Write the capital letter next to each lowercase letter.

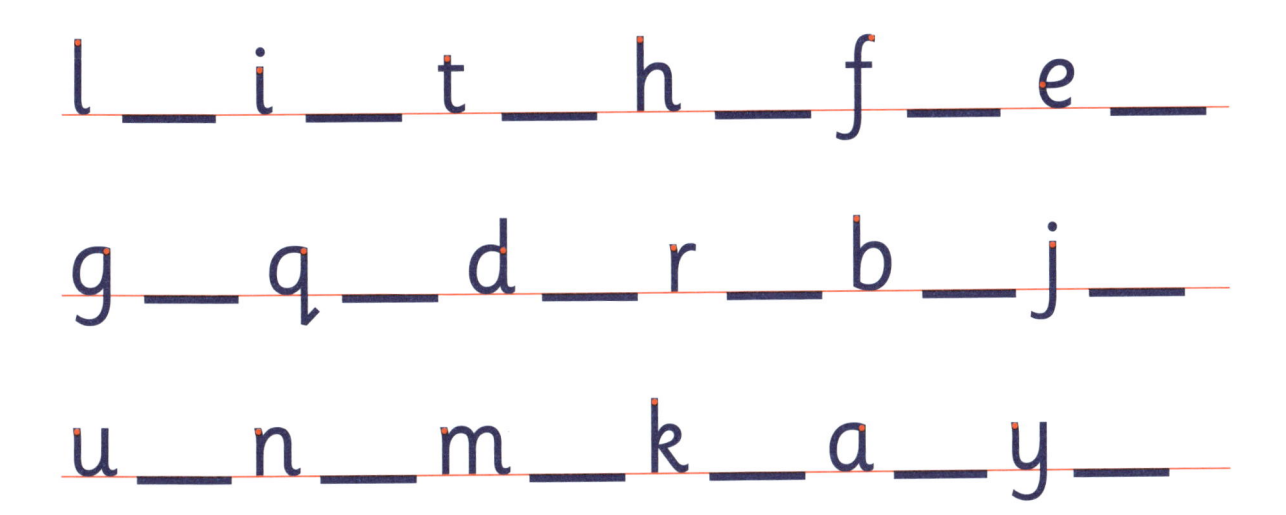

l __ i __ t __ h __ f __ e __

g __ q __ d __ r __ b __ j __

u __ n __ m __ k __ a __ y __

2 Write the capital letters for the letters **c**, **o**, **s**, **v**, **w**, **x**, **z** and **p**.

Apply it

Write each word in capital letters.

yes!

stop!

boo!

ouch!

wow!

moo!

Book 4 | Capital Letters and Numbers

WriteWell challenge 1

Write the numbers to complete the rhymes. Use your best writing.

I wiggle 8 fingers.
I wiggle ___ ___ toes.
I wiggle ___ shoulders.
I wiggle ___ nose.
I wiggle my hips 1 2 ___.
No more wiggles left in me!

1, 2, 3, ___, ___
Once I caught a fish alive.
6, 7, ___, ___, 10
Then I let it go again.

1, 2, buckle my shoe.
3, ___, knock at the door.
___, ___, pick up sticks.
___, ___, do not be late.
___, 10, say it again!